SOUTHDOWN ANCILLARY VEHICLES

SIMON STANFORD

AMBERLEY

First published 2022

Amberley Publishing
The Hill, Stroud
Gloucestershire, GL5 4EP

www.amberley-books.com

Copyright © Simon Stanford, 2022

The right of Simon Stanford to be identified as
the Author of this work has been asserted in
accordance with the Copyrights, Designs and
Patents Act 1988.

ISBN 978 1 4456 9605 8 (print)
ISBN 978 1 4456 9606 5 (ebook)

British Library Cataloguing in Publication Data.
A catalogue record for this book is available from
the British Library.

Origination by Amberley Publishing.
Printed in the UK.

Introduction

Ancillary vehicles, or fleet support vehicles as they are sometimes referred to, form a fleet of miscellaneous transportation used by bus companies to back up their operational bus and coach fleet. Bus and coach company ancillary fleets would include vans and lorries to attend roadside breakdowns, deliver spare parts to depots or for bus stop maintenance, and those used for publicity. Recovery tenders, some converted from former service buses, would recover broken down buses or worst still those involved in accidents. Driver training buses were former service buses converted for the role. Buses converted to publicity or information centres, mobile information trailers, driver restrooms, left luggage offices, and fuel tankers all make up the ancillary or support fleet.

Southdown Motor Services operated an impressive and interesting array of these varied vehicles. Recovery tenders were Leyland TD5s: new as double-deck buses in the 1930s, later replaced by AEC Matadors and Bedford 'Green Goddess' trucks from the 1950s, and finally Leyland and Daf towards the end of the Southdown era, all serving the company admirably for many years. Vans and lorries were of British Leyland and Ford manufacture, as were many staff cars. Driver trainers were Leyland PD2 and PD3 Queen Marys converted in-house at Portslade works. A surprise acquisition in 1983 was an AEC fuel tanker – now in preservation. Long-serving tree lopper 421 DCD served in this role for many years around the Southdown area and was also loaned to other national bus companies until her replacement came in the form of a Bristol VR. Two elderly single-deckers from the 1940s served as left luggage offices, as did a Northern Counties-bodied Leyland Leopard, and a Bristol RE was a drivers' restroom at Uckfield. The 1979 fleet list of Southdown, as an example, includes forty-five ancillary vehicles and thirty-seven staff cars spread across the depots.

Some survive in preservation with private owners or museums, regularly on display for us to see and reminisce over, and the model manufacturers have produced fine die-cast replicas for us to collect.

Nowadays, in bus and coach company fleets the support vehicles are significantly reduced. For example, recovery is carried out by contractors in most – if not all – firms, training buses are in lesser quantities, there is no longer a need for fuel tankers, and one hardly ever sees a converted bus as a restroom or office of any description.

This book is a pictorial history and a tribute to a respected and innovative company, and while photographs of their ancillary fleet are somewhat elusive many friends and fellow enthusiasts have helped to bring together a selection of pictures and information in the captions, which cover as many of the 100 years of Southdown as possible. I have added some variety to the book and included other vehicles becoming ancillary or support vehicles with other operators, including some with a connection to Southdown or the area in which they operated.

The oldest Southdown ancillary vehicle to feature in the book is lorry L2. She is a 1932 petrol-engined Leyland Tiger TS4 originally fitted with a thirty-two-seat Harrington body. Requisitioned by the war department between 1940 and 1946, Southdown reacquired her *c*. 1947 and built and fitted the lorry bodywork as seen in the picture. Operating on trade plates, she would deliver parts to all the Southdown depots. By 1965 she was parked up out of use at thirty-three years old. She reportedly still survives in some form. Thanks to the Southdown Enthusiasts' Club for photo and information. (SEC)

A pair of 1947 Leyland PS1 single-deck buses with ECW bodywork served as left luggage offices after withdrawal from passenger service. GUF 729 was fleet number D691 in this ancillary vehicle role. After withdrawal she was stored at Portslade works and remained on the fleet list as late as *c*. 1984, surviving a remarkable thirty-seven years. She lasted until *c*. 1999 and was broken up for spares.

The second 1947 Leyland PS1 to serve as a left luggage office at Bognor was HCD 449, issued fleet number D689. It is pleasing to see her today in preservation at the age of around seventy-three years old. Beautifully restored by the late Bob Gray.

An old black and white photo from the mid-1960s shows us the pair of Leyland PS1 rear-entrance half-cab coaches new to Southdown in 1947 serving as left luggage offices at Bognor depot. (PM Photography)

Another view of Bognor depot and the pair of Leyland PS1 rear-entrance buses in use as left luggage offices. GUF 729 faces us in this view and HCD 449 has her back to us. (Peter Dann collection/SEC)

Bristol K at the rescue. A wonderful Old Steine, Brighton, scene. Brighton Hove & District breakdown tender running on trade plate 111AP converted from a Bristol K5 double-deck bus. (M. King collection)

Breakdown tender W4 running on trade plate 162AP. Southdown-BHD fleet name is evident in this view in Brighton on her way to the aid of a stricken bus somewhere. Alongside this Bristol K is an early Leyland National from the 1973 batch. (John Fozard)

EAP4 a 1948 Bristol K double-deck bus new to Brighton Hove & District in 1948. A driver trainer in 1962, she was converted to a recovery vehicle in 1965 and became part of Southdown in 1969 as fleet number W4 painted green with Southdown – BH&D fleet names. She was withdrawn c. 1974 and sold to a preservationist, completing twenty-six years' service in three different guises. Photographed outside of Conway Street depot, Hove. (Courtesy of Bristol Vintage Bus Group)

The ancillary fleet included vans allocated to the publicity department of Southdown and were used to travel around all the depots and bus stations to update timetables, signage and associated advertising. One such van allocated to this duty was SUF 982. This old image was taken at Uckfield bus station. (Peter Dann collection/SEC)

A wonderful view of Edward Street garage in the late 1950s/early 1960s and a Leyland PD2 (OCD 770) dominates this picture. To the left is RCD 610 fleet number V10 – a Morris J type van reported to serve the company for seven years. A fine replica of this make of Southdown van can be seen further on in the book. (PM Photography)

The oldest driver training bus to feature in the book is Brighton Hove & District 6442, a 1952 Bristol KSW (GPM 902) with bodywork by Eastern coachworks. New in 1952, she was part of the fleet acquired by Southdown in 1969 and converted for the role that year and allocated fleet number T442. Withdrawn in 1976 and sold to a dealer, she was scrapped in 1977. (Southdown Enthusiasts' Club)

0827 is of a type typically used by the military, formerly a gun tractor and somewhat rare in the Southdown recovery fleet. Described in the company fleet list as a 'Ford Canada breakdown lorry', she was allocated to the Worthing area. She ran on trade plates 097BP and 338PX. This view was taken *c*. 1973 and her replacement followed two years later. Oxford Diecast produced a fine replica of her in Southdown livery. (Michael Hitchen)

Converted to a breakdown tender from a Leyland TD5 bus and seen here in Hilsea depot in September 1964 operating on trade plate 172BK. (J. S Cockshott archive; Mike Eyre)

Southdown did all publicity in-house and a number of vans were allocated around the depots for this task. A Portsmouth shot of V72, a Ford Thames publicity van taken in August 1967. Note the use of advertising space on the side. (J. S Cockshott archive; Mike Eyre)

Fleet number V63 was a Ford Thames 400E van allocated to the engineering department at Edward Street garage, Brighton. This close-up shot taken in Pool Valley depicts the fine detail applied to company vans. Oxford Diecast produced an exact replica of this van in 2013. (Peter Dann collection/SEC)

Oxford Diecast produced a superb 1:43 scale model of Ford 400E van in 2016. The detailing is as precise as can be, including the registration and fleet numbers and advertising on the van sides. Ancillary vehicles are a welcome addition for model collectors.

Land Rovers added more variety to the ancillary vehicle fleet and was a versatile vehicle to have to hand, dealing with most vehicle emergencies on the roadside. Fleet number L12 running on trade plate 420BP was photographed in Worthing garage in 1984. Looks like they are bus lights fitted to the front. (Nigel Lukowski)

Southdown Leyland TD5 breakdown tender on trade plate 184CD at the rescue of a Brighton Hove & District Daimler Fleetline near to Brighton's Old Steine. Southdown took over BH&D in 1969 and the Fleetlines new in 1969 and 1971 remained in BHD livery until repainted. (Remember When)

A superb old view of Southdown's busy Eastbourne garage with Leyland TD5 breakdown lorry operating on Eastbourne-issued trade plate 150HC. I imagine she is returning from a rescue mission or about to embark on one. (John Law)

Converted from a 1938 Leyland TD5 double-deck bus to a breakdown tender and allocated to Eastbourne depot where this photo was taken in June 1968. Originally EUF 198 she became 0198 in the service vehicle fleet. (Robert Hendry)

Leyland TD5 breakdown tender 0198 running on trade plate number 067HC and earning her keep recovering Leyland PD2 MCD 746 in her home town of Eastbourne in April 1963. (Richard Maryan)

EUF 198, a Leyland TD5 breakdown tender in colour. Remarkably, this old girl survives in preservation carrying her original registration number once again. She has achieved a remarkable eighty-two years and remains active. (Remember When)

I have broadened the term ancillary or service fleet to include this magnificent old image of a Southdown caravan or mobile booking office, situated close to the Palace Pier in Brighton probably in the late 1950s or early 1960s. Used to promote and take bookings for coach holidays and excursions. (Peter Dann collection/SEC)

Southdown led the way in promoting bus services and coach travel in any way possible. This caravan is at the Bluebell Railway in May 1984 and no doubt Southdown would have all manner of leaflets and brochures for anything from local bus services to holidays by coach. The Ford Transit van towing the caravan is HWV 917V fleet number V17 and allocated to Brighton. (Southdown Enthusiasts' Club)

The die-cast model manufacturers did not overlook Southdown's use of caravans. Oxford Diecast produced this excellent quality 'booking office trailer', as they aptly described it when released in 2017.

In Southdown traditional livery is this 1966 Ford Transit van FCD76D fleet number V76 photographed in Edward Street garage, Brighton, *c*. 1967 only a couple of years after the Transit was produced. The sliding doors and wing mirrors are a reminder of days gone. (Peter Hirst)

Ford Transit Van FCD 78D fleet number V78, photographed *c.* 1969. Close examination of this image reveals the period advertising for extended tours and private hire and on the door is 'Engineering Department Worthing'. Note the addition of a roof rack and the Southdown scroll fleet name below the bonnet where the Ford badge would have been. Interesting detail added by the company. (Peter Hirst)

One of many Ford Transit vans purchased by Southdown over the years. Fleet number V87 was a Brighton-allocated engineers' van. This August 1969 photo was taken in Pool Valley, Brighton. (Mike Street)

Ford Transit van OUF 88G was new in 1968 and allocated to Portslade works. A year later Southdown became part of the National Bus Company and V88 received the rather bland National white livery, losing the familiar green and advertising. (Michael Hitchen)

A 1969 van purchase was RUF 590H, the familiar Ford Transit 18 cwt fleet number V90 – one of three in that year. Allocated to Portslade works, it remained on the fleet until around 1980. (Michael Hitchen)

The third one of this trio of Transits from 1969 is RUF 592H fleet number V92 allocated to the engineering department in Portsmouth and photographed in one of the garages in that area. In green livery with the addition of a National Bus Company badge on the front grille. (Michael Hitchen)

A view of Ford Transit van V98 in her home town of Brighton looking a little worse for wear, no doubt soon to be replaced by a newer model. Behind is a Triumph car from the period and a Devon general AEC bus. (Michael Hitchen)

Brighton-allocated Ford transit van V98 from the 1970s, seen parked at the well-known Pool Valley bus and coach station. (Southdown Enthusiasts' Club)

Ford Transit JPN 271N fleet number V1 of two identical vans from *c.* 1975 replacing earlier models and allocated to the Brighton area – typical multipurpose vans used around the garages. (Michael Hitchen)

A 1973 purchase was Mini Van ECD 806L fleet number V96. Allocated to the Brighton area, these small vans made ideal inspectors vans. That could well be its use here in this Pool Valley, Brighton, view. (Michael Hitchen)

The Mini Van quantity only reached around five, with Southdown in the 1970s not remaining in the service fleet quite as long as their Ford counterparts. This small van was an ideal size for inspectors use or publicity. V3 is outside the Pevensey Road bus station, Eastbourne.

There is around forty-two years between these two recovery tenders. Leyland TD5 EUF 184, previously a 1938 double-deck bus converted for her ancillary use. STW 356W is a DAF 2800 bought in by Southdown to replace the ageing Bedfords, subsequently passing to Stagecoach. Both are proudly on display at the Southdown centenary event in 2015.

A distant shot of restored and preserved breakdown tender EUF 182 heading a line-up of attendees for the 'Southdown 70' celebrations in 1985. Converted from a 1938 Leyland TD5, she was an impressive forty-seven years old in this view.

Brighton-allocated breakdown tender 0181, seen here in the town showing her traditional green and cream to great effect. Hard to believe she was new in 1938 as a double-deck bus. She was replaced after nearly twenty years on the service vehicle fleet. (Peter Dann collection)

A close-up image of one of the former Leyland TD5 buses converted to a breakdown tender and seen here in Brighton. Study this image it reveals the fine detail such as the Southdown scroll badge and the resemblance to her days as a bus from the cab. (Peter Dann collection)

A close-up view of breakdown tender 0184 running on trade plate number 339PX at Bognor depot. The National Bus Company era is upon us – evident from the badge on the front grille. (Peter Dann collection)

0184 EUF 184 was new to Southdown in 1938 as a double-deck bus with bodywork by Beadle. Converted to a breakdown tender in 1957, she was photographed in 1984 by Paul Llewellyn in Horsham depot, where she spent her later years. (Paul Llewellyn)

It is 1988 in Horsham depot and 0184 is looking somewhat down at heel, now withdrawn from service when photographed by Paul Llewellyn. She had completed fifty years of sterling service and is now deserving retirement. (Paul Llewellyn)

Home is the Southdown garage at Amberley Museum, near Storrington, West Sussex, for 0184. Still active in retirement and attending many events, such as the London to Brighton run and various events held in the museum grounds. (Taken at Amberley Museum)

A rear view of EUF 184 looking magnificent – hard to believe she is well over seventy years old and a pleasure to see preserved. Taken at Amberley Museum during one of my many visits to the bus event held there each year.

New in 1967, Marshall-bodied Leyland leopard HUF 769E takes a tumble on the way to Brighton on service 117 in May 1969, ending up at a precarious angle. Dispatched to recover bus 169 is AEC Matador 0826. (PM Photography)

The badly damaged Leopard safely behind a very capable machine, AEC Matador JNG 641 breakdown lorry fleet number 0826. The Matador joined the ancillary fleet in the late 1940s and was still in use around the early 1980s. (PM Photography)

A magnificent view of the mighty matador no doubt making light work of towing the damaged Leopard. In this view they are approaching the Old Steine, Brighton, presumably en route to Portslade works. (PM photography)

The AEC Matador is a mighty and very capable vehicle and it is brilliant that so many survive in preservation, having been restored to high standards. Formerly 0826 in the service fleet registered JNG 641. There is no mistaking where she is parked: Maderia Drive, Brighton. She is taking part in the London to Brighton historic commercial vehicle run.

Bedford recovery tender 0829 moved to Hampshire bus at Winchester in Stagecoach ownership, as seen in this 1992 view. Originally NYV 372, she ran on trade plates during her time with Southdown. A change in the law saw the Bedfords reregistered, with this one becoming Q99 2AFG. (Paul Llewellyn)

Eastbourne-allocated breakdown tender 0830 seen in the Cavendish place depot displaying trade plate 242HC. This Bedford S type is freshly painted in this 1970s view alongside a Leyland Leopard in Towsend Thoresen livery new in 1976.

Having a rest inside Cavendish Place, Eastbourne, keeping Leopard 1843 company is 0830, running on trade plates 242HC. One of three Bedford SHZ green goddess recovery vehicles purchased to replace elderly Leyland TD5s dating from the late 1930s. (Southdown Enthusiasts' Club)

Bedford SHZ recovery tender 0830 operating on trade plates 242HC from Eastbourne recovers accident damaged Leyland Leopard NUF 452G from High Hurstwood in April 1981. Ironically, the Leopard would join the ancillary fleet, as seen further on in this book. (Paul Llewellyn)

A rear view of Leyland Leopard NUF 452G on tow behind the Eastbourne recovery tender 0830. Note the lighting board and recovery trucks number plate in the rear window of the Leopard, and the narrow lane in which the recovery has taken place. (Paul Llewellyn)

Originally NYR 459, this is Eastbourne's Bedford breakdown tender 0830 busy again, this time attending a failed Leyland National number UFG 47S near Friston, East Sussex, in May 1982.

Eastbourne-allocated Bedford 0830 changes identity slightly in this 1989 image, becoming Q99 5AFG and formally operating on trade plate number 242HC. She is rescuing Leyland National number 118 near Lewes in March 1989. (Southdown Enthusiasts' Club)

Portsmouth-based Bedford SHZ recovery tender 0831 rescues a defective Leyland Leopard coach fleet number 1320 at Battersea coach park, London, in the late 1980s. Operating on trade plates 333BK, the original registration mark was NYV 495. (Richie B.)

An authentic replica of a 1959 Morris J van. Original Southdown examples do not exist; this example is beautifully restored to replicate the original Southdown vans of this type and era. Seen at Winkleigh in 2013.

The Morris J type van on display at Southsea in June 2015 to celebrate the centenary of Southdown. Corgi made a die-cast model of the Morris J van in fleet livery – an exact replica of the type used.

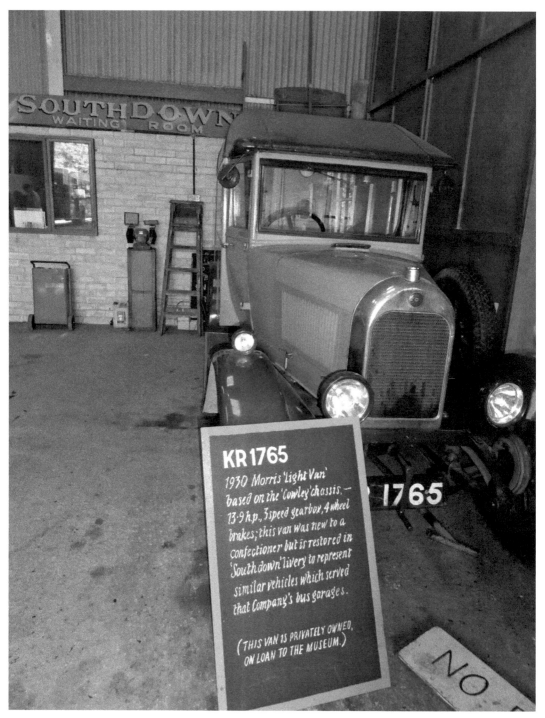

A 1930 Morris light van taken at Amberley Museum on one of my many visits. New to a confectioner but restored in Southdown livery, replicating a type that is certainly not out of place and could easily be a Southdown ancillary vehicle. Features of this van are a 13-horsepower engine and five-speed gearbox.

A close up of this authentic 1930 Morris van in Southdown livery. A lovely addition to the collection at Amberley Museum. Taken by Paul Llewellyn in 2007. (Paul Llewellyn)

An amazing addition to this photographic history of Southdown ancillary vehicles is early tree lopper GUF 161. A 1945 Guy Arab fitted with Gardner engine, she was converted to a tree lopper in 1955, renumbered to 0461 and withdrawn in 1969. Note the workmen in full uniform and not a hi-vis in sight! (Peter Dann collection/SEC)

Tree lopper RUF 183 was a 1956 Leyland PD2 with Beadle bodywork receiving conversion work for the role. Numbered 0783 and allocated to Eastbourne, she would be loaned to depots as tree-lopping work around the Southdown area was required. This view is at Fareham depot *c.* 1973. (Michael Hitchen)

An October 1975 view of Beadle-bodied Leyland PD2 tree lopper 0783 parked up posing for the camera. (Peter Dann collection/SEC)

May 1981 at Bognor depot with Queen Mary tree lopper 0421 some four years into her support vehicle role and looking in fine fettle. Also in the view we see a rare rear-view image of Bristol RE number 235. (Nigel Lukowski)

421 DCD, a convertible open-top Queen Mary was a long-serving member of the service fleet as a tree lopper, being converted for this role *c.* 1977 following a low bridge accident. Numbered 0421, she was often loaned to other NBC companies. Photographed in Maidenhead with Alder Valley in the July of 1983. (Neil Gow)

Few companies had their own tree lopper, which made 0421 sought after. This time she is loaned to London Country and was photographed at Warlingham, Surrey, in 1987 by Alan Edwards. (Alan Edwards)

Rear-view shots are priceless when recording a photographic history of buses. 0421 rear end received some modifications; for example the registration plate was relocated to where the route numbers used to be. (Thanks to Alan Edwards for this 1987 shot in Warlingham)

Is this the most photographed ancillary vehicle? I think she is, and why not. A full frontal of 0421, this time taken during her stay with London Country, helping to keep bus routes free of overhanging trees. (Thanks to Alan Edwards)

0421 hard at work in East Sussex between Framfield and Uckfield on a cold February day in 1988 – about the eleventh year into her tree-lopping career. (Paul Llewellyn)

A rear shot of 0421. Note the road sign attached to the rear door warning approaching motorists of the road narrowing. Looking at the overhanging trees in this photo, a daunting task is ahead. (Paul Llewellyn)

Leyland PD3 Queen Mary 954, new in 1964, spent the first eight years of her Southdown career promoting holidays in Sussex. Suitably adorned with advertising material and information, this role took her to various locations in the UK and to northern France too. This view taken at Portslade works *c.* 1966 sees her prepared for a trip to France. She survives today beautifully restored and preserved. (Peter Dann collection/SEC)

Following a low bridge accident in 1996 former Southdown Bristol VR JWV 251W became a tree lopper with Stagecoach south, carrying fleet number 15751 and looking the part following the conversion work. She is seen in anger in January 2015 at Fairlight while on loan to East Kent. Southdown Enthusiasts' Club)

On display at the Southdown centenary event at Southsea in 2015 is tree lopper JWV 251W. She was sold not long after this photo was taken, ending her days as spare parts for another Bristol VR. (Southdown Enthusiasts' Club)

A line-up of former Southdown Bristol VR buses with tree lopper JWV 251W showing her rear end and the conversion work that took place. Sadly, her tree-cutting days were nearly over when I took this photo in 2015 at the Southdown centenary event.

Sad times ahead and 0421 is looking rather down at heel following her demanding career as a tree-lopping bus spanning some eighteen years. Seen here after donating her registration to another bus and becoming PRX 458B. Photographed in Lancing, West Sussex, July 1995 in company with a former Southdown Ford lorry and not long to go before the Queen Mary was scrapped. (Thanks to Steve Vallance)

By far my favourite vehicle in the service fleet was YJB 271J, fleet number 0832, a Leyland Retriever recovery truck. A new addition to the recovery fleet *c.* 1980. Some conversion work being carried out in-house at Portslade works and the crane was fitted by Wreckers International. Photographed in Dover July 1983. (Southdown Enthusiasts' Club)

On display at Amberley Museum in May 1982 is Leyland Retriever 0832, purchased to update the recovery fleet in more heavy duty form. Allocated to Conway Street depot, Hove, she would be called to recovery Southdown buses and coaches as required but also come to the aid of other National Bus Company operator's vehicles. (Peter Dann collection)

The formation of Brighton & Hove bus and coach company led to the transfer of a portion of the Southdown fleet included YJB 271J, the Leyland Retriever recovery truck. Numbered G18 and looking resplendent in her new owner's colours, she is seen near the Conway Street depot in 1986. (Southdown Enthusiasts' Club)

Former Southdown and Brighton & Hove Leyland Retriever survives today in preservation, albeit in a different form minus the crane. Photographed a long way from her former south coast home at the East coast run, Hull, around 2010. My thanks to Pete for his help with this one.

DAF recovery trucks were purchased to replace the ageing Bedford SHZ type and continued into Stagecoach ownership after the purchase of Southdown in 1989. Southsea in June of 2015 is the date and location of STW 356W, in attendance at the Southdown 100 event.

STW 356W, first of a trio of DAF recovery trucks and the last breakdown trucks bought by Southdown. Allocated fleet number R1 in Southdown ownership. Hilsea depot is the location for this April 1989 shot. (Nigel Lukowski)

UHK2 12W fleet number R2. In Stagecoach ownership these DAF trucks were repainted in Stagecoach striped livery, thus losing the Southdown green and cream livery. (Thanks to Alan Conway)

DAF recovery truck HDP 438W was fleet number R3. Photographed inside Worthing garage in 1989, the same year Stagecoach purchased Southdown. (Nigel Lukowski)

A 1976 lorry purchase was a Leyland Terrier dropside, replacing an older Ford D series of similar size. Allocated to Portsmouth, this view was taken at Portslade and it was no doubt used for collecting spare parts from central stores. (Southdown Enthusiasts' Club)

A close up of Ford D series lorry L1 smartly turned out in green and cream complete with Southdown scroll badge on the front grille. A batch of four were purchased around 1980 and allocated to the main depots.

Four Ford D series 3-ton lorries came in to the service fleet in the late 1970s, replacing similar but older models. Parts transportation was their primary use. HUF 902V fleet number L2 was allocated to Eastbourne, and is photographed at the Cavendish Place depot. (Southdown Enthusiasts' club)

Southdown's fleet of vans served a variety of uses: for engineering breakdowns, parts collection, publicity and bus stop maintenance. HWV 914V is a Leyland 440 EA van fleet number V14. A Conway Street vehicle is being used for bus stop maintenance in this view. (Nigel Lukowski)

Fleet number V22 is a Ford Transit mobile workshop based on the parcel van and similar in type to the sixteen-seat minibus of that era. This van would have used in locations such as London to provide back up for the many coaches coming in and out of the capital and provide cover for events such as the Epsom Derby where high volumes of Southdown vehicles would attend. (Nigel Lukowski)

Fleet Number V20 was the engineering service van based at Haywards Heath where I worked back in the late 1970s and 1980s and recall many miles covered in this van attending breakdowns or collecting parts. This 1986 image was taken in Perrymount Road, Haywards Heath, opposite the former bus station site. (Southdown Enthusiasts' Club)

After the closure of Haywards Heath garage the small workshop facility was reopened at Lewes bus station and Ford Transit van V20 became based there, losing the East and Mid Sussex decals and National Bus Company badge from the front grille.

Vanguards model van released by Lledo Vanguard *c.* 2004 in 1:43 scale is this fine Southdown Ford Transit van in green and cream livery. Based on the Mk 1 Transit it is still a welcome addition to Southdown's ancillary history.

Included on the 1985 fleet list was another trio of Ford Transit vans. This purchase was high-back parcel vans used for a variety of tasks. B25 JFG was V25 in the ancillary fleet and allocated to Eastbourne. (Michael Hitchen)

Leyland PD2 T765, a Worthing-allocated training bus, seen outside Portslade works in 1977. Four from this 1955 batch of Park Royal-bodied buses became trainers *c.* 1970, initially in green and cream until adopting the standard yellow and white colours. (Paul Llewellyn)

Hayling Island depot was used to store surplus vehicles or those due for disposal. T765 was photographed there in September 1978, although remained on the fleet list until 1981. (Paul Llewellyn)

T768 initially joined the driver training fleet in Southdown green and cream before being painted yellow and white. This 1972 view was taken in Freshfield Road, Brighton, near to the Southdown head office and garage. (Peter Dann/SEC)

A wonderful shot along Marine Parade, Brighton, of smartly turned-out 1955 Leyland PD2 OCD 768 fleet number T768. Seen passing the aquarium and a line-up of cars we remember from the 1960s. Britbus produced a superb die-cast model of this bus.

Leyland PD2 training bus T768 is twenty-one years old in this view taken in Eastbourne in 1976, and very smartly turned out too. (Southdown Enthusiasts' Club)

Britbus excelled here with their 2011 release of Leyland PD2 training bus T768. The detailing is second to none – an authentic addition for Southdown model collectors.

Southdown driver training buses were former service buses converted in-house for their new role. T769 is a 1955 Leyland PD2 with Park Royal bodywork. One of four of this batch converted for training, she was replaced in the early 1980s, putting in a sterling twenty-five years' service. (Nigel Lukowski)

Portsmouth-allocated Leyland PD2 driver training bus T772 in very much out of passenger service condition. This photograph was taken in September 1972. She remained green and cream for about four years before a repaint to yellow and white. (Peter Dann collection)

A superb shot of driver trainer OCD 772 outside of Uckfield bus station and garage. Still in green and cream livery with the addition of the double-N symbol applied to all National Bus Company vehicles. (Southdown Enthusiasts' Club)

A very presentable T772 at Conway Street garage, Hove, on one of my trips to the depot. She was one of sixteen buses in the training fleet at the time – *c.* 1979. This Leyland PD2 is a survivor in preservation restored to traditional green and cream livery.

Taken in March 1979, Leyland PD2 training bus poses for the camera in Eastbourne, although some of her training bus career was in the Portsmouth area. (Paul Gainsbury)

Former training bus OCD 772 in preservation and restored to traditional Southdown green and cream. 772 was thirty years old when photographed by Paul Llewellyn at Amberley bus show in September 1985. (Paul Llewellyn)

A pair of the 1961 Queen Mary training buses parked at the Conway Street depot in 1980. Hard to believe they are nineteen years old in this view. There is the usual high standard of presentation and it's hard to tell the difference between them. (Paul Gainsbury)

T872 is a Queen Mary that was new in 1961. Along with three others from this batch she was converted and painted in the yellow and white livery *c.* 1975 for her new role. Photographed outside of the Conway Street Hove depot where the majority of the training fleet were allocated.

June 1978 at Conway Street depot is the location for this view of Queen Mary training bus 287 7CD fleet number T877 taken by Paul Llewellyn. The fleet list in this year included eleven driver training buses. (Paul Llewellyn)

An Old Steine, Brighton, view of Leyland PD3 Queen Mary driver training bus before her passenger survey bus role displaying the local garage advertising to great effect. (Peter Dann collection)

Parked outside Worthing garage in March 1985 is T880, taking on her passenger survey bus role and remaining in yellow training bus colours. This Queen Mary dates from 1961 and is twenty-four years old in this view. (Southdown Enthusiasts' Club)

A May 1985 view of training bus T880 in Chichester bus station taking a slightly different role as a passenger survey bus retaining her advertising for a car dealership. She would be used for this purpose all over the Southdown operating area. This was a temporary allocation as withdrawal was imminent. (Southdown Enthusiasts' Club)

Sad times ahead at Horsham depot in May 1987 with a cull of withdrawn and surplus vehicles. Included was former 288 0CD, the 1961 Queen Mary having been a driver training bus and latterly a survey bus. With her original registration donated to a coach she is now XUF 467A and awaiting collection by a dealer. (Paul Llewellyn)

The 1979 Southdown fleet list saw the addition of Leyland PD3 Queen Mary FCD 292D fleet number 0292 to the ancillary fleet, becoming the market analysis project bus. In this view she largely retains her NBC green and white livery.

Southdown's central repair workshops were in Victoria Road, Portslade – one of the most fascinating places I have ever been. On display at their open day in 1983, and looking nothing other than immaculate, was FCD 292D, the market analysis project bus converted by the central works staff to the usual high standard.

Passenger survey bus 0292 was not camera shy in the 1980s. She would be used from all the depots within Southdown as required, and photos record a view of the depots long since demolished and all but a memory. Hailsham garage is the location of this photo in March 1985. (Southdown Enthusiasts' Club)

0292 outside Pool Valley in May 1985. By 1990 this Queen Mary passed to Stagecoach with the purchase of the company and continued a similar role as a mobile office and conference room and was painted in Stagecoach corporate livery. (Southdown Enthusiasts' Club)

September 1987 and one of the most photographed ancillary vehicles. 0292 is in Hove looking resplendent with a fresh coat of paint, losing the rather drab grey to the upper deck. (Southdown Enthusiasts' Club)

0292 continued her ancillary role in the 1990s after the purchase of Southdown by Stagecoach. She is looking striking here in Stagecoach stripes, seen on display at North Weald bus rally in 1990.

The Southdown depot in Cavendish Place, Eastbourne, is the setting for this view of Queen Mary training bus 0292 in Stagecoach corporate livery when photographed by Richard Maryan in February 1990. T294 is behind still in green and cream livery. (Richard Maryan)

T293 parked up at her home depot, Conway Street depot, Hove, in March 1983. Southdown's achievement in presentation and standardisation is evident once again in this view. (Paul Llewellyn)

Driver training buses were seen at all the Southdown depots as part of the training regime. FCD 293D fleet number T293 was photographed outside of the Whitehawk, Brighton, depot in June 1985 – the seventieth year of the company. Note the appropriate logo next to the fleet name. (Paul Llewellyn)

Pool Valley, Brighton, is the location for this view of T293. New in 1966, she became a driver trainer joining four Leyland PD3 Queen Marys from this batch in the late 1970s. She was sold to a dealer *c.* 1991 and presumably scrapped. (Garry Donnelly)

T294 is one of five, an FCD batch of Leyland PD3 Queen Mary buses to join the ancillary fleet as a driver trainer. Looking smartly turned out when caught by the camera in Brighton April 1982. (Southdown Enthusiasts' Club)

T294 was allocated to the Hampshire division of Southdown when this 1986 photograph was taken in Cosham. This Queen Mary survives in preservation restored in green and cream. (Paul Gainsbury)

A pair of driver training buses parked up at Conway Street depot, Hove. Leyland PD3 Queen Mary T295 was new as a service bus in 1966 and one of the Leyland PD2s was new as a service bus in 1955. (Peter Dann collection/SEC)

I would have to make numerous trips to Portslade and Conway Street during my time working for Southdown. Queen Mary training bus T295 was parked up in Conway Street on one such visit *c.* 1980. After withdrawal by Southdown, Shamrock and Rambler acquired her for further use in their ancillary fleet as a training bus.

Victoria Road, Portslade, was the location of Southdown's central repair workshops. During their open day in September 1983 Queen Mary training bus T295 was posing for the camera, with many enthusiasts recording this event. She was one of a dozen driver trainers on the fleet during that year. (Peter Dann collection)

Not an ancillary vehicle when this black and white photo of FCD 295D was taken, but a reminder of how the Queen Mary double-deck buses looked when in abundance in Brighton. This photo is of great interest as it is taken at the bottom of St James's Street where the National and British Rail travel offices are visible and 295 is working a 37A service – a former Brighton Corporation route. (Southdown Enthusiasts' Club)

The training fleet could be seen in use all over the Southdown area. FCD 296D, fleet number T296, was photographed in Worthing. All of the Queen Mary training buses from this period carried advertising for a local car garage.

Leyland PD3 T296 was allocated to Eastbourne when this photo was taken in 1990 on a bright February day in St Leonards. The advertising for a car garage as carried by all the training fleet was slightly revised. (Southdown Enthusiasts' Club)

Another photograph of T296 in Eastbourne from 1990. In this driver's side view of the bus Southdown's innovation is evident, shown by utilising advertising space on the training bus fleet. Note the hissing Sid logo next to the fleet name. (Southdown Enthusiasts' Club)

T296 photographed on Maderia Drive, Brighton, in June 1985, forming part of the '70 Years of Southdown' display. After disposal, a non-PSV role at a school in East Sussex was found for her before being scrapped in 2001.

One of four panoramic Queen Marys joining the ancillary fleet as a driver trainer *c*. 1980 is T360, in very much out of passenger service condition apart from the necessary alterations for her new career. Photographed at Conway Street, Hove, depot.

Driver training bus T360 photographed by Paul Gainsbury in February 1988. In this offside view we can see the additional window and seat fitted behind the driver for the instructor's use – part of the conversion carried out to most Queen Mary trainers. Two upper-deck windows are also blanked out. (Paul Gainsbury)

T360 was transferred to Hampshire Bus in Stagecoach ownership, as seen here at Winchester depot. Other than a change of fleet name and number she is largely the same as her Southdown days, still retaining the garage adverts. Stagecoach livery was later applied, continuing her driver training role in Hampshire. (Courtesy of Richard Vogel)

T362 looking very smartly turned out, freshly painted in the standard yellow and white livery in the training bus fleet. Southdown, as ever, was very innovative, putting advertising space to good use even on their ancillary fleet. (Nigel Lukowski)

Four of the 1967 batch of Queen Marys joined the driver training fleet in 1980, initially used in their NBC green and white livery. Repainted in yellow and white and carrying advertising for a local garage is HCD 364E, becoming T364 and seen at Conway Street depot in 1984. (Southdown Enthusiasts' Club)

A February 1980 view of Queen Mary trainer T365, newly allocated to the driver training fleet to replace the Leyland PD2 buses. She initially retained the National Bus Company livery. Palmeira Square, Hove, is the location. (Peter Dann collection)

T365 looking immaculate in this 1983 photo outside Southdown's central workshops in Portslade – a credit to the company achieving this level of presentation. 365 was sold to Northern Scottish *c.* 1985 where she continued as a driver trainer for a short time. Further non-PSV use continued until the inevitable – the scrap man – in 2002. (Southdown Enthusiasts' Club)

March 1983 and driver training bus 365 is posing for the camera at Conway Street depot, Hove. The National Bus Company chairman's award symbol for innovation is evident in this view alongside the fleet name. Southdown won this award in 1981. (Paul Llewellyn)

Bristol VR 514 was not originally destined to join the ancillary fleet, nor was it worthy to include this one. Having had a light refurbishment, including repaint into the East and Mid Sussex livery, she suffered early withdrawal after mechanical failure. Donating some parts to other vehicles, she became a store at Hailsham garage. (Nigel lukowski)

In January 1986 Bristol VR 510 begins a short-lived driver training career with Brighton & Hove still carrying Southdown fleet name. Looking good for fifteen years old, she was withdrawn in July 1987. (Nigel Lukowski)

Brighton & Hove bus and coach company acquired three convertible, open-top Queen Marys from Southdown for use as driver training buses in 1988. Seen outside their Conway Street garage in 1990 is T1, originally 405 DCD, painted cream with black mudguards and bearing similarities to the open-top fleet from a bygone era. Belgium became her home after somewhat bizarre alterations. (Paul Llewellyn)

Leading a trio of Brighton & Hove training buses is T3, originally 407 DCD with Southdown. Relatively short-lived as a driver training bus in Brighton fleet, the three Queen Marys were sold in 1991. This one reportedly was exported to Germany for further use *c.* 1994. (Paul Llewellyn)

A 1989 addition to the Brighton & Hove driver training fleet was a former Burnley Leyland PD2 seen outside the Conway Street garage in cream and black livery to match the three former Southdown Queen Marys. The Leyland double-deck training buses were replaced around 1991.

Bristol RE NUF 439G was taken from the service bus fleet in 1981 for conversion to a drivers' crew room, situated in Uckfield station yard. A diesel-powered generator was mounted in the engine bay to provide electricity. Numbered '0439', it would remain in this role until *c.* 1987. (Paul Llewellyn)

Another view of 0439 in the ancillary vehicle fleet. Uckfield was an outstation and the bus provided facilities for drivers' rest breaks. Maintenance on the generator was carried out by engineering staff at Haywards Heath depot and the author took many trips to Uckfield to maintain it. (Paul Llewellyn)

A bleak winter in Uckfield with a snow-covered station yard. 0439 and the service buses no doubt iced up, there would have been and a visit from the engineers at Haywards Heath to help out. (Paul Llewellyn)

Earlier in the book we saw the Eastbourne recovery tender towing a Leyland Leopard after an accident in April 1981. NUF 452G was the casualty. Merely a month or so later, after a basic repair to the bodywork, the seats were removed and she became the left luggage office at Eastbourne depot, retaining fleet number 3113. The end came in 1986 when she was scrapped. (Paul Llewellyn)

A mere six months after sustaining accident damage, former 452 became a permanent resident in Cavendish Place depot, Eastbourne, as a left luggage office. This black and white shot was taken in October 1981. (Paul Llewellyn)

Based on the Bedford TJ range, this van is in the fleet of Brighton Hove & District in their red, cream and black livery. It is seen parked outside the Conway Street depot. This range of vans were manufactured from *c.* 1957, dating this photo around the early 1960s. (Thanks to Mike from Remember When photography)

Bristol VR UUF 115J transferred to Brighton & Hove in 1986 along with six other early flat-screen Series 1 buses. Some became driver training buses for a time before withdrawal. 115 is seen in the Old Steine on a wintry February day in 1986. (Nigel Lukowski)

A former Yorkshire Traction Leyland national NHE 406M, fleet number G19, was converted to a mobile travel shop by Brighton and Hove in 1986. It is seen on display at the 34th British Coach Rally on Maderia Drive, Brighton. It left the ancillary fleet by 1990, completing just four years in this role.

The Stagecoach purchase of Southdown in 1989 not only brought their corporate livery to the south coast but different vehicle types too. Queen Marys, as driver trainers, become a thing of the past. GLS2 65N, 0265 in the ancillary fleet, is an Alexander-bodied Leyland Leopard and takes up the training bus role. Originating from Scotland, she is caught posing for the camera at a bus rally in 1992 at Apps Court.

During the National Bus Company era companies in the NBC Group would provide roadside assistance if there was a breakdown in their area, even supplying a replacement vehicle on occasions. London Country have helped Southdown by recovering a Duple-bodied Leyland Leopard with their AEC tow truck and bar towing the coach to the safety of Chelsham garage in Surrey. (Thanks to Alan Edwards)

A rear view of the Southdown Leopard, in National Express livery, being given a helping hand by the London Country AEC. These trucks were common among bus companies, with many converted from tipper trucks or tankers.

Brighton Corporation ran a fleet of buses alongside Southdown in the town and their ancillary vehicles were of great interest, including this Leyland Beaver recovery truck dating from 1973 and photographed at the Lewes Road depot. It was common in this period to run on trade plates, but 1988 saw this lorry revert back to its original registration. (Thanks to Steve Vallance)

Brighton Corporation purchased two Daimler Fleetlines from London Transport in 1980 and put them to use as driver trainers. Fleet number 91 was EGP 132J – new in 1971 and still on their fleet list in 1990. She survives in preservation, restored to original London Transport red. Photographed at Netley Showground in 1990.

Former Southdown AEC Mammoth Major fuel tanker DLK 292C, fleet number 0833, having been purchased by John Murphy for restoration in 2017. The following pictures show us some of the work John has done to the tanker.

Getting a lift on a low loader to her place of restoration.

John means business as the cab is removed as part of a full restoration.

Looking rather down at heel, but wait no longer as truck enthusiast John Murphy restores this AEC to her former glory.

The restoration continues with a full mechanical and body makeover.

There is some catching up to do. Former Bristol Omnibus Leyland Octopus DLK 125C is restored by John Murphy.

Looking fairly complete and ready for some paint.

Repainted and pretty much finished – looking superb. She took part in the 2019 Trans Pennine run.

As good as new! This former Southdown tanker poses for the camera – a remarkable restoration and a credit to John.

Another finished view of John Murphy's wonderfully restored former Southdown fuel tanker.

Convertible, open-top Queen Mary, formerly 404 DCD, was not a driver training bus in her Southdown days. United Counties acquired her for this purpose and she certainly looked well presented when on display at Amberley in *c*. 1990.

None of the convertible, open-top Queen Marys served as ancillary vehicles with Southdown. Around eleven did elsewhere, however, including 419D CD, becoming YRC 182 with Trent in Derby from 1988 to 1996, marketing their training school as Tiger Training. Former 419 received some modifications, such as an instructor's opening window behind the driver and side indicators. After withdrawal by Trent she returned south for preservation, reunited with her original registration.

A bus with a history worthy of inclusion is Bristol FLF FPM 73C, new to Brighton Hove & District in 1965 and becoming part of the Southdown fleet in 1969. After withdrawal in the late 1970s she became part of the United Auto ancillary fleet as a driver trainer and would be seen in the Newcastle area in the early 1980s. Her career as a driver trainer continued with Clydeside in Scotland as their fleet number JT5 until withdrawn and scrapped in 1989 following an accident when she left the road, ending up on her side.

LFS 297F is an early Bristol VR with a history. New to Eastern Scottish in 1968, she was one of eight acquired by Southdown in 1973 in exchange for Bristol Lodekkas. She was numbered '545' with Southdown and allocated to Haywards Heath during my time there. By 1981 she was one of at least three of the batch transferred to Eastern National for driver training. This photo was taken at their Southend depot. (Thanks to Mark Wilson)

Numerous Southdown buses and coaches have become driver training buses and ancillary vehicles with other operators upon disposal. One such bus is Leyland National WYJ 169S, new to Southdown in 1978. Twenty-three years later she appeared at North Weald bus rally looking very smartly turned out as a driver training bus with MK Metro.

Plaxton-bodied Leyland Leopard coach 179 DCD was withdrawn from the Southdown coaching fleet *c.* 1977 to embark on a role in the ancillary vehicle fleet. Retaining fleet number 1179 she was repainted in a yellow livery, complete with engineering training vehicle decals, and joined the training school based at Portslade works. She would be used to take apprentices to Tile Hill College in Coventry up until *c.* 1981. Some alterations to the seating were made with tables fitted. She was reportedly loaned to the college after use by Southdown. (Thanks to Ian Richardson)

Acknowledgements

Gathering material for this pictorial history of ancillary vehicles in the Southdown fleet was no easy task, as many of their wonderful vehicles never met the camera. Only too often the service fleet would be tucked away in the corner of a depot until needed, thus missing the opportunity to be photographed. With the help of many friends and fellow enthusiasts who have searched their photo collections I have managed to compile a selection of images spanning a forty-plus-year period of Southdown.

My sincere thanks to Paul Llewellyn, Paul Gainsbury and the Southdown Enthusiasts' Club, Peter Dann, Richard Maryan, Nigel Lukowski, PM Photography, Alan Conway, Bristol Vintage Bus Group, Michael Hitchen, M. King collection, Mike Eyre (J. S. Cockshott archive), Mike at Remember When, Mike Street, Robert Hendry, Neil Gow, Alan Edwards, John Fozard, Peter Hirst, John Law, Garry Donnelly, Richard Vogel, Steve Vallance, Richie B., Mark Wilson, John Murphy for his restoration history of the fuel tanker, and to Amberley Museum for permission to use images taken on their premises. My apologies if I have left anyone out.